CUTE & EASY

Girls!

CAKE TOPPERS

Cute & Easy Cake Toppers for Girls
Birthday Parties or Celebrations!

Contributors

Following a career in finance, Amanda Mumbray launched her cake business in 2010 and has gone from strength to strength, delighting customers with her unique bespoke creations and winning several Gold medals at various International Cake Shows. Amanda's **Clever Little Cupcake** company is based near Manchester, UK: **www.cleverlittlecupcake.co.uk**

Amanda Mumbray

Angela Morrison

Angela Morrison grew up in Venezuela around a wide variety of food and desserts, but it was when she moved to Virginia Beach, Va that her business 'Cakes by Angela Morrison' was born. She has a wide online following for her super cute cake topper creations and her work has been published in many cake magazines and blogs.

Lesley Grainger has been imaginative since birth and has baked since she was old enough to hold a spatula. When life-saving surgery prompted a radical rethink, Lesley left a successful corporate career to pursue her passion for cake making. Lesley is based in Greenock, Scotland. Say 'hello' at: **www.lesleybakescakes.co.uk**

Lesley Grainger

First published in 2015 by Kyle Craig Publishing

Text and illustration copyright © 2015 Kyle Craig Publishing

Editor: Alison McNicol

Design and illustration: Julie Anson

ISBN: 978-1-908707-63-5

A CIP record for this book is available from the British Library.

A Kyle Craig Publication

www.kyle-craig.com

Contents

Welcome!

Welcome to **'Cute & Easy Cake Toppers for GIRLS!'**, the latest title in the **Cute & Easy Cake Toppers** Collection.

Each book in the series focuses on a specific theme, and this book contains a gorgeous selection of beautiful cake toppers perfect for any little girl's birthday party or celebration!

Whether you're an absolute beginner or an accomplished cake decorator, these projects are suitable for all skill levels, and we're sure that you will have as much fun making them as we did!

Enjoy!

Fondant/Sugarpaste/Gumpaste

Fondant/Sugarpaste – Ready-made fondant, also called ready to roll icing, is widely available in a selection of fantastic colours. Most regular cake decorators find it cheaper to buy a larger quantity in white and mix their own colours using colouring pastes or gels. Fondant is used to cover entire cakes, and as a base to make modelling paste for modelling and figures (see below).

Modelling Paste – Used throughout this book. Firm but pliable and dries faster and harder than fondant/sugarpaste. When making models, fondant can be too soft so we add CMC/Tylose powder to thicken it.

Florist Paste/Gumpaste – The large and small shoes in this book are made using florist paste as it is more pliable than fondant, but dries very quickly and becomes quite hard, so it is widely used for items like flowers that are delicate but need to hold their shape when dry.

Florist Paste can be bought ready made, or you can make at home by adding Gum-Tex/Gum Tragacanth to regular fondant.

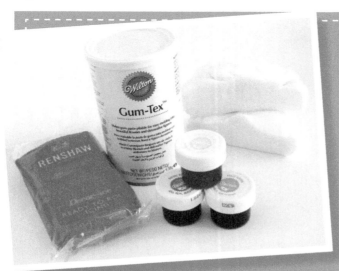

How to Make Modelling Paste

Throughout this book we refer to 'paste', meaning modelling paste. You can convert regular shop-bought fondant into modelling paste by adding CMC/Tylose powder, which is a thickening agent.

Add approx 1 tsp of CMC/Tylose powder to 225g (8oz) of fondant/sugarpaste. Knead well and leave in an airtight freezer bag for a couple of hours.

Add too much and it will crack. If this happens, add in a little shortening (white vegetable fat) to make it pliable again.

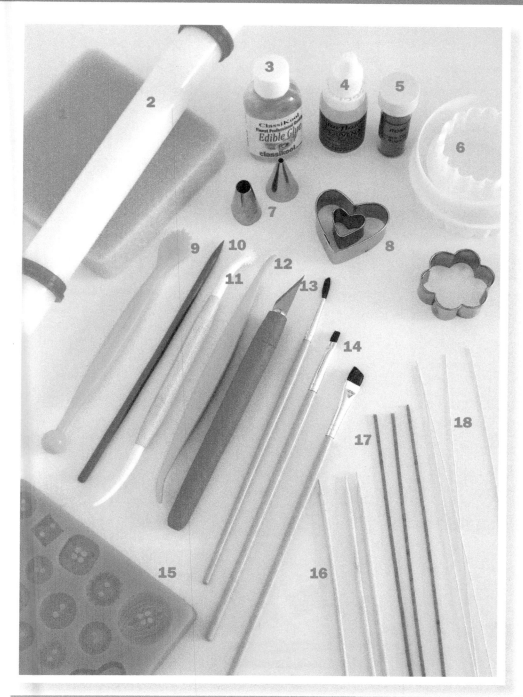

1 Foam Pad – holds pieces in place while drying.

2 Rolling pin – acrylic works better than wooden when working with fondant/paste.

3 Edible glue – essential when creating models. See below.

4 Rejuvenator spirit – mix with food colourings to create an edible paint.

5 Petal Dust, pink – for adding a 'blush' effect to cheeks.

6 Round and scalloped cutters – a modelling essential.

7 Piping nozzles – used to shape mouths and indents.

8 Shaped cutters – various uses.

9 Ball tool/serrated tool – another modelling essential.

10 Small pointed tool – used to create details like nostrils and holes.

11 Quilting tool – creates a stitched effect.

12 Veining tool – for adding details to flowers and models.

13 Craft knife/scalpel – everyday essential.

14 Brushes – to add finer details to faces.

15 Moulds – create detailed paste buttons, fairy wings and lots more.

16 Wooden skewers – to support larger models.

17 Spaghetti strands – also used for support.

18 Coated craft wire – often used in flower making.

Edible Glue

Whenever we refer to 'glue' in this book, we of course mean 'edible glue'. You can buy bottles of edible glue, which is strong and great for holding larger models together. You can also use a light brushing of water, some royal icing, or make your own edible glue by dissolving ¼ teaspoon tylose powder in 2 tablespoons warm water. Leave until dissolved and stir until smooth. This will keep for up to a week in the refrigerator.

Making Faces

The faces featured in this book vary in terms of detail and difficulty. If you're a complete beginner, you may opt to use simple shapes and edible pens to draw on simple features. As your confidence grows, you can use fondant for eyes and pupils, edible paint for features, or combine these methods for some great detailing.

 Various colours of paste can be layered to create detailed eyes.

 Edible pens can be used to draw on simple features.

 A tiny ball of paste can create a nose.

 Black fondant with white fondant or non-pareils make detailed eyes.

 Pink petal dust adds blush to cheeks.

 When adding tiny pieces of fondant for eyes, use a moist fine brush.

 An extruder can be used to make hair!

When making small figures for cupcakes, it's great to place each on a topper disc, and place this on top of a lovely swirl of buttercream. This way the figure can be removed and kept, and the child can tuck into the main cupcake.

Regular round cutters are essentials, and there are also a great selection of embossing tools and sheets out there that, when pressed into your rolled paste, will create cool quilting effects on your disc. Make your discs first and allow them to harden before you fix your figures to them.

Some figures may use a toothpick or skewer for support, so be sure to take care with these around small children.

Plunger cutters are a great way to add cute details to your models. They cut and then 'push' each small piece out, making it easy to cut small flowers, leaves and shapes.

Painting Details

Many of the projects in this book have beautiful details painted onto the mini items. Mixing regular gel or paste food colouring, or lustre dusts, with rejuvenator spirit will create edible paint in any colour you need. Keep a small collection of fine paintbrushes handy too!

Coloured details – mix your regular food colouring with rejuvenator spirit to create edible paint.

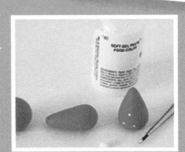

White paint – Americolor Bright White gel paste colour is strong enough to paint on clear white details.

Materials

Modelling paste:
Pink; pale & dark
Blue
Green
Yellow
Grey
Brown
Black
White
Lustre Dust; pink
8 Rice Krispie bars
Edible Glue

Tools

Craft knife/scalpel
Veining tool
Cone tool
Scallop tool
Kemper texturising tool
Fine paintbrush
Toothpicks
Circle cutter
Pastry circles
Daisy Cutters

1 First, let's make a cute stable for our ponies!

2 Arrange the cereal bars and stick together using a little edible glue.

3 Slice away a sloping roof.

4 Cut out panels to fit the sides of the stable.

5 Mark ridges with the edge of a ruler, and mark on the wood grain pattern using a veining tool.

6 Attach them to the cereal stable.

7 Continue to attach the panels to the sides. Cut a front and rear panel and add wood effect here too.

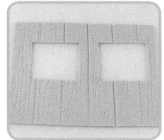

8 Cut out two square holes in the larger front panel.

9 Cut a rectangle of black paste large enough to cover the two holes and stick on the underside.

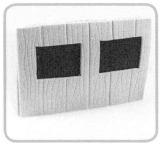

10 Attach it to the front of the stable.

11 Make a panel for the roof, marking out roof tiles.

12 Conceal the joins with some contrasting coloured edging.

13 Attach the roof.

14 Roll out a long sausage to make the stalk of the sunflower.

15 Flatten two teardrop shapes of paste and mark on leaf details with the veining tool.

16 Cut out two daisies and stick together.

17 Make a centre for the sunflower, adding texture with a toothpick.

18 Place two toothpicks in the stable doors ready to take the pony heads.

19 Now let's make our lovely little ponies, one of each colour!

20 Roll out a ball, stretching to an oval and indenting slightly in the centre.

21 Use a ball tool to make the eye sockets, a paint brush to make holes for the nostrils, holes ready to insert the ears, and a little mouth with the scallop tool.

22 Flatten two teardrop shapes, and insert into the holes.

23 Add a couple of flattened balls for the eyes, and a very thin strip for the contrasting fur on the forehead.

24 Paint in the eyes and dust the cheeks with a little petal dust.

25 Add a little strip of paste for the harness, and make two little imprints with a piping tip.

26 Attach the head to one of the toothpicks.

27 Roll out a few tear drop shapes for the mane and attach to the top of the head.

28 Make a further horse, in a different colour if desired.

29 Now for a rosette for the birthday girl!

30 Cut out a scalloped circle.

31 Using the bulbous cone tool, roll it back and forth over the edge of the circle to frill it.

32 Make a second circle and stick them together.

33 Attach a circle in the centre.

34 Cut out two rectangle shapes with a craft knife, cutting away a little V at the end of each strip.

35 Attach these to the back of the rosette.

36 Add your birthday girl's age.

37 Let's give our ponies a bucket of water to drink!

38 Cut out a little circle.

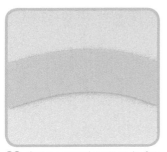

39 Cut a curved rectangle for the sides of the bucket.

40 Moisten the edge of the circle and wrap the sides around the base of the bucket.

41 Attach a little strip around the top edge of the bucket.

42 Add a little strip for the handle and allow to dry.

43 They must be getting hungry by now!

44 Make two rectangles out of paste.

45 Use the texture tool to make the rectangles look like hay.

46 Add a fine sausage of paste for the hay ties to finish.

Materials

Modelling paste:
White
Red
Orange
Yellow
Pink
Green
Purple
Blue
Edible Glue

Tools

Craft knife/scalpel
Butterfly cutters (various sizes)
Round cutters
Paste extruder
Foam drying mat
Heavy gauge florist wire

1 Bend a length of florist wire into an arch shape. This will be used to add support to your rainbow. We used gumpaste for this as it will dry nice and hard.

2 Cut a circle of white paste not wider than the width of your cake.

3 Cut a smaller circle from the centre...

4 ...and cut in half. Use a rolling pin to slightly stretch each semi-circle downwards, creating a deeper rainbow shape.

5 Place your florist wire on top of one of the semi-circles of paste, spread the whole area with edible glue, then sandwich the remaining piece on top.

6 Create balls of paste in all colours of the rainbow! Again, we used gumpaste as it dries harder. (We'll also use some to make the butterflies later).

7 Use a paste extruder to create the first roll of paste for your rainbow. You can also carefully roll this by hand, ensuring it is an even sausage.

8 Start with the smallest arc of colour, attaching this to your dried support with edible glue. Continue to attach each different colour.

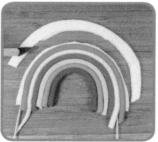

9 Before attaching the final strand, remove any unwanted excess paste with a scalpel tool.

10 Complete all colours, allow to dry then repeat on rear. Dry fully before attaching to cake.

11 Roll differing sized balls of white paste and arrange in a cloud shape. Allow to dry.

12 Roll a thin layer of white paste and drape over your cloud, gently shaping and tucking to create a 'covered' cloud.

13 Cut butterfly shapes in a variety of sizes from your rainbow coloured paste. Allow to dry 'in flight' on a foam drying mat.

14 Glue the butterflies to your cake in a sweeping formation, and position rainbow and clouds on top as shown.

Rainbow Cupcakes

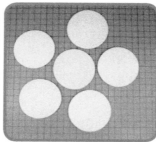

1 Cut 6 topper discs to fit on top of your cupcakes – 4 x white and 2 x pale blue. Dry until firm.

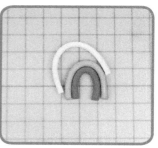

2 Use extruder tool, or roll by hand, to create coloured strands for your rainbow. Start from the smallest length...

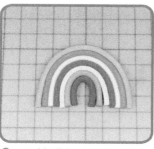

3 ...and build outwards, gently attaching the strands together. Measure as you go against your topper disc and trim to fit.

4 Attach the rainbow design to the topper disc with edible glue, and add 'stitching' detail with your edible ink pen.

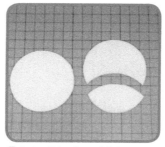

5 Cut a thin disc of light green paste, same size as other topper discs. Use the edge of your cutter to 'split' the disc, as shown.

6 Attach the smaller piece to the bottom of a pale blue topper disc.

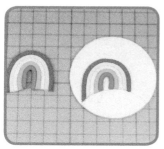

7 Create a small rainbow, as shown in Steps 2-3. Use your round cutter to cut at a slight angle to fit the 'hill'.

8 If you don't have a cloud cutter, use a large blossom cutter instead. Cut a white blossom then make another cut further down, as shown.

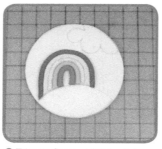

9 Trim to fit your little rainbow landscape design.

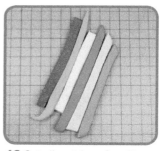

10 Cut slim strips of multi-coloured paste.

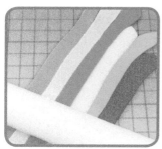

11 Gently roll together, ensuring that the pieces remain tightly packed alongside each other.

12 Cut a slightly smaller circle from your length of striped paste. Attach to centre of a white topper disc.

13 Attach the child's age in white paste. Add stitching detail with edible pen.

14 Cut a small plaque and add the child's name in a contrasting colour and mount on a striped disc, as before. Now you have a cute set of cupcakes!

1 Our little Snow White is just too cute to eat!

2 Slide a little column of sugar paste for her bodice on to a moistened toothpick and leave to dry upright for at least 24 hours, or until set.

3 Roll a ball for the head.

4 With the end on the ball tool, make hollows for the eyes, and add a little ball for the nose.

5 Add ovals of white paste for the eyes.

6 Roll a very fine sausage of paste for the eyes lashes.

7 Add more paste for the pupils of the eyes, a small nose, and paint on the mouth. Dust the cheeks with a little pink petal dust.

8 Add a circle of paste for the hair.

9 Cut a strip of red to make the alice band.

10 Roll out the shapes above to make the hair.

11 Arrange the hair on the head, and mark with a veining tool. Add a little bow.

12 Add a little strip of yellow paste down the front of the dress.

13 Insert the pick into a cupcake iced in bright yellow (the skirt).

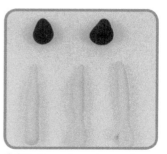

14 Roll teardrop shapes for the sleeves, and open up one end with the ball tool. Roll a tapered sausage and shape end into a hand, as shown.

15 Attach the arms to the cupcake using edible glue.

16 Roll a little apple, making a hole at the top. Flatten a teardrop shape for the leaf, marking on the details, and roll a tiny sausage for the stalk.

17 Arrange the apple and place it on the cupcake. Flatten teardrop shapes and attach to the dress sleeves.

18 This princess is ready to go to the ball!

19 Follow steps 2-7 for the body and head. Attach a circle of yellow paste for the hair.

20 Add a strip for the alice band and two tiny balls for the pearl earrings.

21 Roll a ball for the bun, and an indented sausage for the fringe.

22 Attach them to the head with edible glue.

23 Ice the cupcake, and attach a cut away circle in a lighter shade, as shown.

24 Insert the body and head.

25 Make the arms as in step 14 and attach to the cupcake, and paint sparkles on to the skirt with white gel food colouring.

26 This princess looks just like Elsa!

27 Follow steps 2-7 for the body and head. Attach a circle of paste for the hair.

28 Roll out long tapered sausages and attach to the head, starting at the centre and working outwards.

29 To build up some height, add a few smaller pieces at the centre.

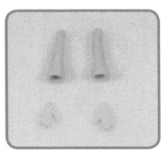

30 Roll out two tapered sausages and open the end of the sleeve with the ball tool. Shape two hands, as shown.

31 Attach the arms to the body and glue the hands in place.

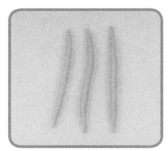

32 Roll out three long sausages.

33 Braid them together, and attach to the head.

34 Paint on a few snowflakes using white food colouring.

35 I wonder if Jasmine has a genie in this little lamp?

36 Follow steps 2-7 for the body and head. Attach a little bra shape to the body.

37 Attach a circle of paste for the hair and add a little strip for the alice band.

38 Roll out two long tapered sausages, and attach to the head.

39 Roll out two teardrop shapes for the earrings.

40 Flatten a ball of yellow, and attach a smaller flattened ball of blue for the amulet.

41 Insert the body into the cupcake.

42 Make the arms as in step 14 and attach them to the body.

43 Roll out a long sausage, taper at both ends, and intermittently along the length. Cut out the required number of strips to cover the tapered sections.

44 Attach the pony tail to the head.

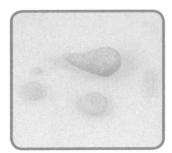

45 Roll out the shapes shown to make the lamp - a teardrop for the lamp, circles for underneath and on top, a small ball for the lid, and a small sausage for the handle.

46 Attach the lamp to the cupcake, and paint on some little twinkles.

Tools

Craft knife/scalpel
Tools; veining, scallop,
ball, Kemper
Pastry circles
Toothpicks
Bamboo skewer
Diamond embossing mat
Fine paintbrush

1 A 'cake' on top of a cake now that's cute! You can use a second real cake here, or a polystyrene dummy.

2 Ice the bottom tier of your cake, and apply the techniques used in step 27 for the drippy icing.

3 Cut a wedge from the smaller cake and decorate the main part as shown.

4 Now decorate the cake wedge - we're using a polystyrene dummy here but you could use the cake wedge you just cut.

5 Ice the top and side of the wedge in your chosen colour.

6 Add some light brown coloured paste to make the cake part.

7 Use the texturing tool to make it look like cake.

8 Roll out a long sausage, purposefully making it thinner and fatter along the length. Attach it to the middle of the cake.

9 Repeat the process with a thinner strip of red for the jam.

10 Roll out a small ball and make a hole in the top.

11 Roll out a fine sausage of green to make the stalk, and insert into the hole.

12 Roll out lots of teardrop shapes, placing them on top of each other.

13 Arrange the teardrops on top of the cake to look like piped frosting.

14 Attach the little cherry.

15 Cut out a circle, removing the centre with a smaller circle cutter. Cut into sections for the eyes. Cut another circle in half for the mouth.

16 Attach the eyes and mouth to the cake wedge as shown.

17 Dust the cheeks with a little pink dust.

18 This little ice cream guy is just the cutest!

19 Roll out a cone shape. Insert a bamboo skewer all the way through and into the cake dummy below.

20 Roll out some paste and emboss it using the diamond embosser. Wrap it around the cone, and leave it to dry.

21 Roll out a ball of paste, and flatten the side on your work top.

22 Turn the cone the right way round, and attach the ball of ice cream.

23 Roll out an uneven sausage of paste.

24 Attach the sausage to the neck of the ice cream, and secure with a toothpick.

25 Roll a couple of teardrop shapes out to make the ice cream look like it's melting and glue in place.

26 Roll out some brown paste, and mark a circle with a pastry cutter.

27 Cut within the circle randomly to make it look like drippy chocolate sauce.

28 Attach the sauce to the top of the ice cream, smoothing down the edges.

29 Make a cherry as in steps 12 and 13, and attach it to the top of the ice cream.

30 Make two sausage shapes, and insert toothpicks into the bottom of each one.

31 Wrap fine strips of brown paste around them in a spiral pattern.

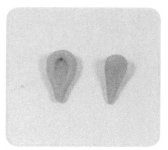

32 Insert the wafers into the top of the ice cream.

33 Make two teardrop shapes, and flatten them in the centre with the wide end of the veining tool.

34 Stick them point to point, and attach a flattened ball of paste for the centre to make a bow.

35 Attach the little bow to the ice cream with edible glue.

36 Paint on a little face using food colouring, and dust the cheeks with petal dust.

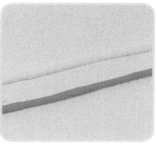

37 Every candy cake needs some lollies!

38 Roll out two long sausages of paste.

39 Twist them together.

40 Coil them up into a spiral, and roll over them with your rolling pin to flatten them slightly. Attach a bamboo skewer to the back with a little glue.

41 And some fruity lollipops too!

42 Attach a ball of paste to a bamboo skewer. Paint it with a little piping gel to make it look shiny.

43 And some too cute to eat candies!

44 Roll out a ball of paste, making two holes in either side of it.

45 Make two teardrop shapes, flattening them with the scallop tool. Insert them into the holes to make the sweet.

46 Decorate them however you like - stripes, polka dots, or even a little happy face!

Candyland Cupcakes

Materials

Modelling paste:
Red, Pink
Yellow, Green
Pale blue
Flesh
Light brown
Dark brown
Black
White
Lustre Dust; pink
Edible paint; various
Edible Glue

Tools

Craft knife/scalpel
Veining tool
Pastry circles
Small daisy cutter
Fine paintbrush

1 Roll out a ball of paste, and either using your finger or the end of a paintbrush, make a hole through the centre.

2 Smooth out the hole in the centre of your donut.

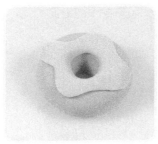

3 Cut a circle of paste, remove the centre and make the edges wavy with your craft knife.

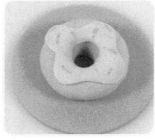

4 Attach the donut to a disc of sugarpaste and paint on some sprinkles.

5 Attach two little balls of paste together, and make holes at the top with the end of a paintbrush.

6 Roll out a sausage of paste, and bend in half. Insert into the top of the cherries and add a line of white paint.

7 Flatten a teardrop shape of paste, marking on the leaf detail with the veining tool. Attach them to a disc of sugarpaste.

8 Make a teardrop shape, and flatten at both ends for the cupcake base. Mark lines up the side with a veining tool.

9 Roll out a long sausage of paste, and arrange it on top of the cupcake to look like frosting.

10 Make a tiny cherry following the steps in 5 and 6.

11 Roll out a teardrop shape.

12 Attach a little daisy to the top and make a hole with the end of a paintbrush.

13 Roll a tiny sausage shape and insert into the hole.

14 Attach to a disc of sugar-paste and paint on the facial details and strawberry seeds.

Materials

Modelling paste:
Red
Pink
Yellow
Pale blue
Green
Black
White
Pale pink
Edible paint: various
Edible Glue

Tools

Craft knife/scalpel
Veining tool
Pastry circles
Extruder
Small leaf cutter
Various piping nozzles
Fine paintbrush

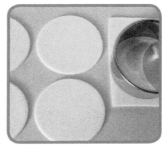

1 Cute one large white topper disc to fit each cupcake.

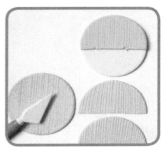

2 Cut half circles and add texture for hair, as shown.

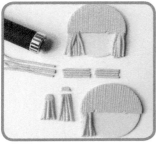

3 Push more fondant through an extruder to make hair and position on each side.

4 Make a cute red strawberry hat and add leaf and seed details.

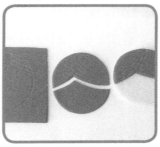

5 Cut the pink hair and add texture with veining tool.

6 Extrude slim strands and wrap around paintbrush and allow to dry before adding to hair.

7 Make a cute 'panda' hat, and texture with the end of a piping nozzle.

8 Use black paste to add ears and eyes, and a ball for white for the nose.

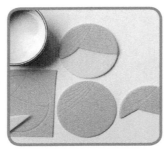

9 Make hair in other colours and add texture as before.

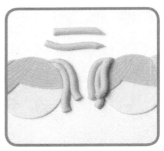

10 Roll thicker sausages and cut to make cute pigtails.

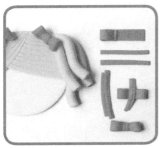

11 Make a cute little bow for each side from strips of paste, as shown.

12 Another new hairstyle!

13 More cute pigtails and bows. Use white edible paint for dots.

14 Finally, add cute eyes and rosy cheeks using paste, and paint on mouth and lash details.

Owl Cupcakes

1 For the first style, cut blue discs for the 'sky', add tiny white spots, and add a section for grass with a scalloped edge.

2 Roll some brown paste into branches, and glue in place, adding tiny leaves.

3 Cut the owl body as shown, add the eyes and a heart to the body area.

4 Use white edible paint to add cute details to the grass, and add small teardrops to form wings.

5 For the next style, cut a brown 'frame' using 2 pastry cutters, and add to a textured disc of paste. Add bow and paint on details as shown.

6 Cut a small owl using various cutters, or with your scalpel, as shown. Add cute flowers to the ears.

7 Cut more cute flowers, small leaves and decorate around the frame area.

8 A new style uses another textured disc, with a cute spotted band across the middle.

9 Cut another little owl shape and add cute paste buttons, as shown.

10 Add eyes and a tiny yellow beak to your owl.

11 Start with another textured disc and add lots of cute little flowers and leaves.

12 Roll brown paste to form a large branch, and add detail to your flowers.

13 Roll two more strips of paste for the 'ropes' of the swing. Add your little owl to the swing.

14 Add a tiny yellow beak to your owl.

Materials

White fondant covered cake
Modelling paste:
Pink – various shades
Edible Glue

Tools

Craft knife/scalpel
Veining tool
Frilling tool
Multi-ribbon cutter
Star cutters
Heart cutters (optional)
Number cutter
Fluted/plain round cutter
Cake pop or lolly stick

1 Cut a large rectangle of paste to create the tiara. Use paper to work out the size best for your cake.

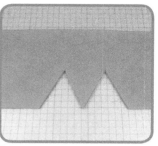

2 Cut the central (and highest) point into the paste with a sharp knife. Cutting the paste facing TOWARDS you (as shown) will be easiest.

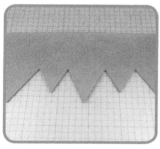

3 Continue to cut two further points, at a lower height than the central one. If you find cutting freehand difficult to judge, see Step 4 for a suggestion.

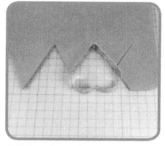

4 Using the pointed end of large heart shaped cutter can be a helpful way to create points in your tiara!

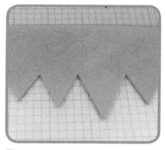

5 When cutting the final points in the tiara, make a deeper cut towards the base of the shape.

6 And when the tiara is turned up the right way, it should look like this!

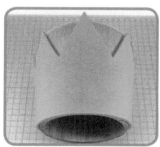

7 Use a cylinder shaped object in your desired size to dry your tiara. Dust liberally with cornflour or use kitchen paper to prevent sticking.

8 Cut a deep star of paste and insert a cake pop stick (or similar) to create a wand. Add interest by indenting with a smaller star cutter.

9 Cut fine strips of dark pink paste using a multi-ribbon cutter (we've used a depth of 3cm). Don't worry too much about the length as the pieces will be discreetly joined.

10 There a lots of ways to create ruffles - we've used a frilling tool. On a firm surface, roll the tip of your tool back and forth at 1cm intervals to create a frill. You can also use a ball tool or edge of a paintbrush.

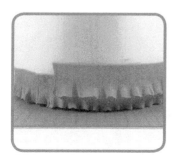

11 Attach the first layer of frills along the base of your cake. Continue to layer subsequent strips in a straight line all the way around, as shown, allowing each frill to be seen.

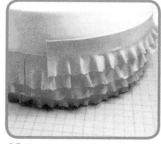

12 To create an ombré effect, simply add some white paste to your pink paste each time you want to make paler strips. We've used three different shades with two lines of each shade.

13 Continue to layer to your desired height and finish with a flat strip of white paste at the top ruffle edge.

14 Decorate your tiara with balls of paste added to each point and an age plaque made using fluted and plain cookie cutters. Add a contrasting star to the wand and other little details as you wish!

Materials

Modelling paste:
Pink – various shades
Pale blue
White
Edible paint; white
Edible Glue

Tools

Craft knife/scalpel
Veining tool
Circle pastry cutters
Large and medium flower cutters
Small round cutter
Small triangle cutter
Toothpick

1 Let's make 4 different styles of cute mini birthday party cupcakes.

2 Cut some plain topper discs then use the large flower cutter and a piping nozzle to make a scalloped flower shape.

3 To make the mini birthday cake, cut a thick round cake shape.

4 For the layered cake, roll out paste in various colours then cut and stack a disc of each as shown. Make 3 of these.

5 Cut a slice from one mini cake and cut another into slices. Save some slices. Arrange as shown, adding some small roses and cream details.

6 Cut some more plain discs to top each cupcake.

7 Now add some cute white spot details to each using the tip of a piping nozzle.

8 Cut some small triangles then roll a white sausage to form the bunting.

9 Add to the disc and add some details with white edible paint and small flowers.

10 Cut strips of paste and form around a toothpick, leaving to dry.

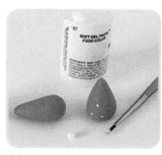

11 Form a small hat shape and add spots of white paint to decorate.

12 Make a little plate from a flower shape, with holes cut using a piping nozzle and a disc in the centre.

13 Form some little cupcakes as shown and place on the plate.

14 Also arrange some small cake slices on plates, and use the hat and spirals to decorate.

Simple Bow Cake

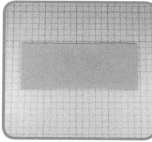

1 Cut a flat rectangle of gumpaste, approximately the width and height you would like your bow to be.

2 Use a stitching tool add detail along the length of the paste, top and bottom.

3 Fold the paste strip over and pinch in the centre of the open end, as shown.

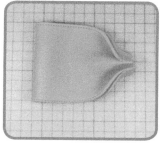

4 Further gather the remaining ends and glue into place.

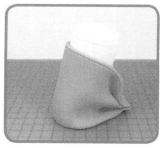

5 Slip some rolled up kitchen towel inside the bow 'loop' and allow to dry. Repeat this process for the other side.

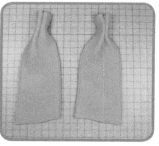

6 Cut two further flat rectangles of paste (adding stitch details) and pinch into a gather at one end, as shown.

7 Place lightly on your cake and trim to fit - cut away excess length and add 'forked' detail and stitch effect at the ends. Press gathered area down to allow bow to sit on top.

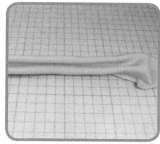

8 Roll a further flat length of paste and pinch loosely into two lengthways folds.

9 Lay this piece face side down, between each loop of your bow.

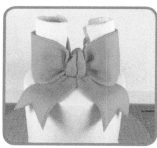

10 Then flip it up and over the join and attach into place, trimming any excess length. Place on top of the tails of your bow.

11 Cut a slim length of paste and add a stitch detail and trim the base of your cake.

12 Cut two contrasting pieces of paste with a plaque cutter. Gently roll the background piece with a rolling pin to lightly stretch it in size.

13 Attach both pieces together (the slightly larger piece will now frame the other one) and add name details.

14 Use a small circle to create polka dots and add to your cake, as shown.

1 To make a striped cupcake topper disc, cut strips of black paste and overlay on a piece of pink paste. Roll to combine, being careful not to distort the lines.

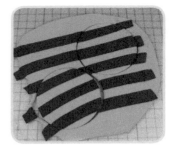

2 Cut a disc for each cupcake from your striped paste. Repeat this with black dots on pink paste (similar to Step 3).

3 Create black and white versions of Steps 1 and 2 by adding black stripes and black dots to white paste.

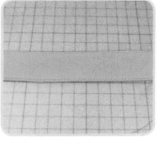

4 To create the large bow, cut a flat strip of pink paste, approx. 3cm x 13cm (1 x 5 inches). Add stitching detail, as shown.

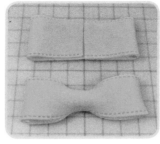

5 Fold over into the middle as shown. Turn the piece over and pinch in the centre, glue to hold its shape.

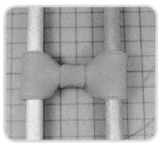

6 Wrap a thin strip of paste over the pinched area. To hold the loops whilst drying, insert supports, as shown.

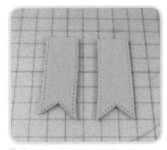

7 Cut two further pink strips and cut forked ends. Add stitch details.

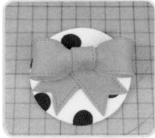

8 Trim to fit a black and white cupcake disc and attach the bow on top.

9 Create a quilted effect topper disc by making a criss-cross design on a piece of flat pink paste.

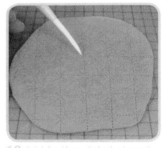

10 Add further detail at each intersection with a veining tool, as shown.

11 Complete by adding the birthday girl's age in a contrasting colour.

12 Cut a small oval plaque from white paste. Add the name in a contrasting colour.

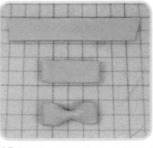

13 Create a smaller version of the bow made using Steps 4 to 6. There's no need to support the loops as this will be much smaller.

14 Add the small bow to your oval plaque and attach to a pink and black topper disc.

More Girly Cake Topper Ideas!

Why not use some of the skills from previous projects to make these cute & easy girly topper ideas?

Pretty Bunting Cupcakes

Summer Berry Cupcakes

Sweet Floral Toppers

RECIPES ♥ TUTORIALS   **Cake & Bake ACADEMY** Est. 2014   RESOURCES ♥ INSPIRATION

Lightning Source UK Ltd.
Milton Keynes UK
UKOW07f1326281215

265383UK00009B/51/P